Archb.

Speaking to God

Translated by
Kevin Christopher Pluchino

Greek Orthodox Archdiocese of America
New York
2012

Greek Orthodox Archdiocese of America
8 East 79th Street, New York, NY 10075
www.goarch.org

©2012 by the Greek Orthodox Archdiocese of America

ISBN: 978-1-58438-024-5   978-1-58438-035-1 (ebook)

All Rights Reserved
Printed in the United States of America

Prologue to the English Edition

This book was written originally in Greek fifty years ago and published in Athens, Greece by the Christian Student Union. Last year the same Christian Student Union published it again in a third edition which was exhausted within weeks. Recently, the book attracted the attention of some people here in the United States, who decided that an English translation would be something truly desirable. Mr. Kevin Christopher Pluchino was kind enough to undertake the work of such a translation. He handily completed the work, and here we have an excellent English translation accurately and handsomely faithful to the original Greek text. He has my warmest thanks for his remarkable contribution.

Times have dramatically changed since 1960 when the book was originally composed. However, when one reads this book today in its English translation, one can see that some basic and substantive human conditions remain exactly the same. Ultimately the need of speaking to God is not affected by any change in time, space, existential needs and social circumstances.

Therefore, I offer this book to our beloved people, especially to the youth, as if it has been written for them, here in America, today. I pray that it will be of assistance in our effort to speak to God, our Father and Creator.

+Archbishop Demetrios of America

New York
October 26, 2011

Introduction

Billions of words are heard every hour upon our planet. They are made up of the substance of every kind of conversations between people.

How many of these words though are addressed to God? How many belong to a dialogue between man and God?

We don't know. That which we do know - from bitter negative experience - is that the dialogues between the inhabitants of Earth and our Heavenly Father must be increased. An urgent need exists for us to have a conversation with Him as the first and foremost element of our lives.

We should speak with God. We should present our problems to Jesus. We should set in front of Him our hard times and our disappointments. We should place our plans, worries, and desires in His hands. This is the meaning and message that this book wishes to bring to the world of our youth, particularly students.

The following pages are not exactly prayers in the usual meaning of the word *prayer*. They are more so attempts at prayer, topics of prayer, and thoughts in prayer. Written in the first person they all can with great ease be placed upon everyone's lips, because more or less they echo, with major or minor changes, those things that each person has in his or her own heart. From this point of view, each reader could simultaneously have been the author of this book.

The First Cycle of this edition contains prayers by which we ask God to teach us how to pray. In the Second Cycle we talk to Him about ourselves and our problems. In the Third Cycle we sing praises of His glory and His majesty. In the Fourth, we entreat Him on behalf of our brothers and sisters, while in the Fifth Cycle the prayers address the need for a true approach to the Gospel.

The reader should not be surprised by the sudden ending of many of the prayers in this book. It is not rare for a conversation with Jesus to remain half-finished. There come times when words cannot express the movements of the soul. When this happens, one's lips are sealed; expressions are almost cut in half. Yet the heart takes it upon itself to continue praying, conversing with heaven, in its own language.

First Cycle

*And it happened when Jesus
was in a certain place praying,
as He finished, one of his disciples
said to Him, "Lord, teach us to pray."*

Luke 11:1

1

I don't know how to pray

My God, I don't know how to pray. Yet I so deeply feel in myself the need for prayer. I want to pray.

Hour by hour the intense longing to talk with You altogether comes over me. The longing to come into contact with You, the Ineffable and Unfathomable. But I lose the words. I cannot piece together what I mean. My thoughts become confused. So often I don't know what to say, while I understand that I have so much to say. Something indefinite, confused, something without shape or form, is in movement within me. A whole world of ideas, feelings, thoughts, and experiences is in a constant tidal wave within me.

I do not want to hide from You, God. In the past years I have prayed but little. From the time I was a child, in my last few years of elementary school, until today, prayer seemed to be almost absent from my life.

Therefore even now that the thirst for contact with You burns me up like fire, I cannot--I do not know how to talk to You. I try to pray, and the same words I used to use when I was a child come to my mouth. But in the condition that I am in today, they seem so strange and foreign that I am embarrassed to use them in prayer.

I beg You, Almighty God: Teach me how to pray. Speak to me. Show me by what divine art I can commune with You. I am sitting at Your feet ready to listen to You. Right now my eyes are fixed only upon You.

The same old question burns my lips as that which Your Apostles asked, *Lord, teach us to pray.*[1]

2

Be the conversant I am looking for

My God, conversation with You is something simple. But at the same time it is also difficult. A dialogue with You, I feel, constitutes the highest art, the most profound science, and the most authentic life.

Oh, how I feel the pressure of being without any training, education, or effort in this direction! God, I feel like an invalid, because up to now no one has taught me the art and method of conversing with You.

I spent many years for my education. I can make myself understood just fine to people who were born in many other places, from places where snow doesn't melt to places where the sun scorches the ground.

I speak freely and comfortably with them. You gave me the ability to have long and interesting conversations with them and with others.

But when it comes time to talk to You, who are my Father who made me, then a terrible weakness comes over me. An odd difficulty engulfs my words. Dialogue with You stops and dies before it begins.

You know, All Wise God, my desire to have a dialogue with You. The wish to converse with You is torturing me. I long to be able to talk to You and for You to answer me. For You to whisper inside me and for me to listen happily and ecstatically.

Lord, I feel a deep pain when I think about how I can go on for hours with my friends and even strangers on serious or empty, meaningless topics while with You I cannot accomplish talking to You even a few minutes, or so often for a second.

I start my day or end it without this supernatural dialogue with You.

Don't leave me, my Savior, in this state any more. Make me a participant in Your living Word. Build up in my contrite spirit and in Your pure and infinite Spirit a bridge of dialogue which my very existence demands.

Become the other Conversant whom I have looked for all these years.

3

Make me feel Your presence

Lord, I have to tell You that prayer is a problem for me. How should I collect my spirit, which is split and squandered in a thousand pieces? How should I concentrate; how can I close off from all around me and within me each entrance from the outside world, appearances, and sensations?

My mind buzzes like a beehive. My ears are bombarded by a million noises. In my eyes images and pictures flash constantly one after the next. And when I close my eyes, my imagination composes and presents me with a sight of many colors.

How should I restrain all of these things, so that I can focus my being and its senses in prayer?

When I speak with someone else, God, I don't need to make a huge endeavor at self-concentration. The other person's presence is felt absolutely. I see him, I hear him, and I hold his hand.

But You, God, I don't see You. You are invisible, inaccessible to our sense of vision. Nor can I apprehend You by my hearing. My five senses betray me. How, then, should I fix my attention on Your face?

They say the only approach to this is through faith. But my own faith is weak and pallid.

Do You see then, God, how hard this attempt is for me? That's why I dare ask You for forgiveness, if so often, for allotting so short a time for prayer, and even then in that time my mind races incessantly here and there, while my soul is besieged by and yields to a whole crowd of things that are completely foreign to prayer.

Empower my faith, O mighty God. Grant me the great gift of feeling Your Presence at the time of prayer. *Show Your face to Your servant.*[2]

Then, I know, the confusion in my thoughts will cease and will stop running toward external things. My soul will be in the clear and beyond any fogginess; its eye will meet the light of Your face, and will be captivated by it.

Oh, that You would have given me this gift! How much more I would have been able to love You then. And how much better would I have prayed….

4

Years without prayer

How could I do such a thing! God, how could I have been so wrong? For so many years to pass without praying?

A life full of storms and feverish moments without the breath of Your contact!

A road fraught with traps, running alongside bottomless pits, beneath tempests, without seeking Your assistance! What folly this was!

I had forgotten You, Lord. I had forgotten my source, my Life. I lived *as one having no hope in the world.*[3] Day by day the human submitted within me. I saw that I was changing into a machine, whenever I did not become an animal. Horrible!

But You felt compassion for me, O Tireless Hunter after souls. You suddenly lit certain brilliant lights in the darkness. I saw.

I perceived that without You everything is futile and loathsome. Suddenly the value and meaning of prayer was revealed to me. Your godly hands parted the ash and mud that covered my heart. You found the spark. You blew on it to fan it. Your breath transformed the spark into a flame.

The fire burns again bright inside me. I thank You.

But the road is long. I still can't pray, my God. I feel tongue-tied. My lips are sealed. I try, but I need Your help.

Stretch out Your hand one more time. Touch my lips. Break the seals, and prayer will gush out like a river from my mouth that until now did not know how to hold the best words for You.

My God, make me a prayerful person. Connect me through prayer with my eternal well.

Second Cycle

The Lord said, "Who among you,
if his son asks him for bread,
will give him a stone?
Or if he asks for a fish,
will give him a snake?
If you then, who are evil,
know how to give good gifts
to your children, how much more
will your Father who is in heaven
give good things to those who ask Him?"

Matthew 7: 9-11

5

I am thirsty for light

My God, I am thirsty for light. I beg for light. I find myself in such confusion, I walk in such a fog, that I have an urgent need of Your enlightenment.

My ideas are indescribably confused. You see what a mess I am inside. Have pity on me.

I have studied in such an undisciplined way, God. I listened with a kind of curiosity that almost bordered greediness. I was often fascinated by modern ideas. I felt myself powerless to the torrential assaults of diverse ideologies.

I lived through the tragic deaths of the different ideals that my soul had embraced.

Now, All-pure Light, I stand in the half-dark twilight like a blind man. I am trembling in my uncertainty. I don't know any more where my next step will lead me, or where my spiritual wandering will terminate.

Open my eyes. *Enlighten my eyes,*[4] Christ. Light up in me the light of Your Spirit, so that I will be able to see correctly, to see fully.

Don't deny me Your light on the path of life. Show me what I have to believe. Set my ideas in order. By Your light burn away in me whatever may be faulty, bad or sick in my spirit. With the brilliance of Your Truth knead my principles and values.

Show me, O Untainted Sun, what I must do, how to live, what I should love, so that I might always find myself under Your bright rays, that I might always be walking *in the light of Your face*.[5]

Please, shine even into my intellect, so that I progress in understanding and I conquer knowledge. Arm my mind with clarity of thought, increase the power of my perception and judgment, and strengthen my memory.

Make me an enlightened person, someone who would always advance in education. The true education.

O Jesus, Eternal Light of the world, *Mark upon us the light of Your face*,[6] and let the brilliance of Your deity shine down on our minds, our hearts, and our wills.

6

Hold my faith upright

My God, my God, hold my faith upright within me. It is shaken. It bows. Doubt - those iron tongs - squeezes my mind all the time. I am afraid that my skull will split into a million pieces.

Unfathomable, Great God, I am being squeezed into the most dramatic contradiction. While I plead with You to support my faith, I act with a shocking composure without faith.

Do You even hear me? Are You there? Maybe I am talking to the air, to absolutely nothing. I am terrified!

My doubts eat my heart. The mind is about to quench the flame in me. My God, hold me firmly. Don't extinguish the light. How will I live without You?

Oh! How many unholy hands sow in my heart the seeds of hesitation and put my faith to the test! Above all, God, the pain that lords over millions of souls staggers me.

Next are my passions, the sub-human that lurks within me, and would even wish that You would not exist.

And the conquests of science, its worship, the inebriation that it brings to mind, all shake the edifice of my faith.

Lord, *increase our faith.*[7] If this was said by the Apostles when they had You near them, and they were physically seeing You and hearing You, what then should I say - I who lives in a confused world, God, where instincts murder reason, the way of life causes nervous breakdowns, and idols hide our vision of You from our weary eyes?

Lord, I believe, *come to my aid in my disbelief.*[8] My Jesus, *increase my faith*. Disperse the cloud of doubt. Make my hesitance disappear.

Give me confirmation of Your presence.

Speak to me. Dispel the silence.

Show me a sign by which my restless spirit may be persuaded to know that You are there.

Hearken to my voice.[9] *And let my cry come to You.*[10]

Lord, I believe, come to my aid in my disbelief.

7

Forgive me

Have mercy on me, God, according to Your great mercy.[11] On my knees before You, Crucified Lord, I beg for mercy, for this grace.

I've sinned. Yet again I've fallen.

I've done exactly the opposite of what Your holy will asked of me. I tasted sin. Its bitter, oppressive taste lingers on my lips.

I am lost. I measure the height of Your holiness against the abyss of my corrupt existence, and I am crushed.

How much filth has piled up within me! My sinfulness chokes me. The fumes from my evil deeds make me almost ready to faint.

Show yourself merciful, my Savior.

You are my Redeemer. You will not let me be destroyed by my remorse. You will be merciful to me.

From the depths I cry out to You, 'Lord, Lord.'[12] Forgive me.

Grant me the delight of the remission of sins. Cleanse me of my iniquity and my sins.

Give me the audacity to gaze at You as I did when I was a child. Clean the filth of my soul.

I implore You kneeling on my knees. Let my tears tell You so.

Lord, I'll wait.

I will not get up, even if my knees bruise and bleed. I won't get up until Your hand touches my bowed head. I will wait until the moment I hear You say: *Your sins are forgiven you.*[13] *Sin no more.*[14]

I'll wait until the hour You wash me in the water of Your Grace. And You will clothe me in the tunics that those who are Your children wear, in the incorruptible raiment of the sons of Your Kingdom.

Have mercy on me, Crucified God.

8

More virtue, more kindness today

Lord, we are thankful for Your love that gave us the gift of a new day. A day that You offered us so that we live, create, struggle, and be glad.

Will something happen perhaps in its duration? Will everyone become richer in good will, like Your divine heart desires? Will the wind bearing healthiness blow upon more people?

I am afraid. God, I am afraid that today crimes will occur, too.

Blood will stain sidewalks.

Injustices will occur today.

The hot tears of those who were wronged, slandered, and despised will water the ground, the stairs of apartment buildings, caverns, and fields. Evil will race madly around the world, break hearts, spread hunger and misfortune, and disrupt households.

And all this - right under Your very sight!

Oh! My soul can't stand it.

God, this evening will the earth weigh more heavily with evil? Will that new day that began increase the amount of sins?

Will You not intervene, O Holy and Righteous Lord?

O Lord of love, let a little less evil happen today.

You have to get in its way.

You have to hinder it.

You have to stop its spread, to make Satan's plans all in vain.

Help us not to be so bad today, so horrible.

Give us strength to create good things, to mold images of goodwill and truth. As it depends on us, extend the area of Your dominion within us and around us. Let there be an abundance of good.

Lord, tonight Satan with his fiery hands will etch on his doomed calendar the account of sins committed here in the world. Couldn't You then mark with Your divine hands in the book of Your Kingdom a rich account of sainthood and good works?

Oh, make me worthy to perform a contribution to this work today.

Lord, please, more virtue, more kindness today.

9

My behavior tortures me

I can't hide from You, Omniscient God. You know how much my behavior tortures me.

I don't act well. My manners show desperate fluctuations. I usually travel between extremes.

My condition oppresses me so much, God, often I exhibit a bad picture of myself.

My relationships with other people are not developing well at all. One day I seem stupidly rude and impolite, and the next day I reach a level of over-politeness.

My own family doesn't know how to deal with me, how to face me. I am their problem, although I don't want to be.

Help me, Jesus, Eternal, Fitting, and Unrepeatable Example of behavior. Fix me.

Plant in my heart the true politeness. A politeness that is calm, proper, and Christian, and that will not degenerate into sweet-sounding words and ridiculous bowings.

Cultivate in me respect and love toward others, fellow workers, friends, relatives, acquaintances and strangers, so that I may talk to them as I ought to, and not hurt them.

Grace me with self-rule, so that I can control my movements and gestures and my words.

That I can govern my temper. That I tame my anger and my excitement, and that I surpass momentary moods.

Please, Lord, teach me a *good behavior*.[15] Guide me in the right direction in mastering it.

Stay by me, my Teacher and Guide of good behavior. And if I make mistakes in how I act, don't turn these mistakes in the direction of provoking clashes and traumatizing my brethren, friends, and fellow human beings.

10

I want so much, I want everything

God, I want so much. See, I want everything. I long to scale the heights of the spirit. But the dizziness that the fall brings fascinates me unimaginably.

What an insufferable dichotomy! A division that loosens colossal powers in me. What torment!

For hours, for days I would like to be an eagle. My heart would mount up to You effortlessly, Lord. It calls for You.

If I could, I'd fly from peak to peak, all at once higher and higher up. So that I might meet You free from everything earthly and sinful. My face drawn by the beauty of Your face would not see anything else.

The world beneath my feet would seem erased, dead. A rubbish heap.

The fall attracts me so much! Satan guides my imagination into places full of the intoxicating aroma of evil flowers. Temptation makes me dizzy.

It seems to me that I am walking on the edge of the roof of a house, and wherever I am I'll fall, and I'll go splat on the hot pavement.

Father of compassion,[16] feel compunction for me. Let this splitting stop.

For so many years the war has not subsided in my chest. At least let some truce be called. Deaden within me the devil's cohort. Give the victory to the one who thirsts for You.

Steady every step of mine that I take to draw near You. Make me more and more Your seeker. Give me the joy of going up to Your summits. Thus the field with marshes and mud will attract me less.

Incomparable Unifier, bring unity in my broken being.

11

Heal me, please

Jesus, what else should I ask from You more than healing? Please release me from the recent illness that is tormenting me.

Outside the sun is shining, my God.

Life is pulsing.

And I am lying down exhausted with a fever and aches waiting for the return of health. I am torturing my own family. They are sick and tired of caring for me in my infirmity. They have high expenses. They are distressed at seeing my illness persist.

Omnipotent Lord, throw off this illness from me for good.

Bend the resistance of the viruses.

Add to the therapeutic power of the medicines.

Enlighten my physician so his diagnosis and the medicinal regimen he follows may be correct and appropriate.

Pick me up, Christ, from my sickbed, which I've been fastened to for so long as if by nails. Shake away my fever. Give me health.

During Your earthly life You healed so many chronic and serious illnesses. *You passed through performing good works and healing.*[17]

So often, Jesus, You had to run, to exhaust Your human self, to reach the sick and give them healing. But as for me, I don't need anything more than one divine word of Yours.

Even that is not necessary. Your wish is enough. When You will it, in the same second I'll be made well.

Come to me then, Incomparable Physician. Put an end to my time of trials.

Heal me, please, I beg You.

12

What shall I do about my finances?

Lord, what shall I do about my finances? I reached a point I can't go beyond. I'm at a loss, and it feels like a belt tightening around me. I feel as if I'm shut in a room without doors or windows. How can I escape?

I did whatever I could, Christ. I set limits to my expenses. I forbid myself from using the bus. My feet have completely worn out. I decreased my meager food budget.

How can I find the money that the continuation of my education demands? How should I proceed? God, my parents have exhausted themselves financially on my behalf. They have been squeezed dry.

It is a shame for me to stop my studies. But again, how can I continue on empty pockets? Money has become a bad dream, a nightmare.

Lord, solve my relentless problem that puts me in agony.

Enlighten me, show me the way, the path.

God, find me a job. Open some door for me.

Put a friendly hand within my own. I am gasping; help me breathe.

You love me more than I love myself. All wise and Omnipotent Lord, if You wish, You can allow me a passage. You can raise up my ruined career and finances.

I depend on You, God. With a nod from You, with an invisible action on Your part, everything will change.

Don't be too late. My need is urgent. I need Your immediate intervention.

Save me from economic ruin. Keep me safe from the claws of despair.

You sustain an entire world, a vast universe. But will You allow my financial problem to go unresolved, God?

13

Reveal my real self to me

Lord, I constantly recognize that I don't know myself. I myself ended up by being the more unknown and hidden from myself.

I am, however dominated by the desire to know myself. But without You I can't accomplish much. So I also call upon Your love.

Reveal my real, true self to me.

Let my sight penetrate everything that I might examine myself in its fathomless depths. I want to investigate my soul as far as its distant corners, and I want to uncover its hidden creases.

O You, *who examine heart and spirit*,[18] don't let life's noises overcome me. Don't let different daily concerns choke me and leave out the saintly work that is getting to know myself.

Help me discover and determine my faults. To become conscious of my weaknesses and vulnerabilities.

Make me see clearly too the advantages You have given me, to be conscious of my strengths, to handle the talents that You have entrusted to me. To learn up to what point my abilities reach and which are the sensitive and vulnerable parts of my heart.

I ask You all these things, Christ, not out of a hollow curiosity, not out of a simple desire to know things. I want to come to understand myself, so that I can fix it, and rejuvenate it. So that I can help in the attempt You Yourself have made to purify and better me.

O Indefatigable, You ceaselessly work within me. You fight in the dark places of my soul in the labyrinths of my spirit. You labor, knock down and build, form and transform my inner world.

And many times I resist! Out of weakness and out of ignorance.

Please, bring me into contact with my real self. Give me courage to look at myself face to face, to study it in a ruthless way. To understand myself however much it may cost.

Lord give me air, give me light in the great diving that I am attempting into the dark, bottomless depths of my existence. Amen.

14

Let me be a warrior for good

Thank You, my God, for adding one more day to my life. This certainly has some meaning, some purpose.

There is something You want from me today, You expect something. But I too don't want to pass my day without purpose. I have decided to be more of a good fighter today. To fight with an irreconcilable insistence, with a steadier passion for everything truthful, just, and holy.

I ask You for help and support.

I implore You, don't leave me to try this alone.

I am usually just as You know me, irritably soft and sluggish. The struggle scares me. I find ways to avoid it. And later I bring a lot of excuses to cover up the shameful flight.

Please, Jesus, take me out of such a condition of laziness. You, O Living God, warm my heart, inflame it. Strengthen my muscles.

Wherever I am today, make me worthy, Omnipotent God, to be a warrior for good. At every moment I should be a defender of justice and a guardian of truth. At home, on the road, on the bus, at work, at university, everywhere.

O Benevolent King, crown my head today with the crown of sweat for the good fight.

Put in me the soul to confront evil and falseness.

Give me the understanding that I have to wrestle with evil, that I have the responsibility to do this. Empower me in the spiritual battle, keep me unyielding in concrete circumstances that will present themselves to me.

Today, at least for today, my God, I want to belong honestly and without reservations to the army of those who fight alongside You for the coming of a better day to our planet.

15

I want to discuss with You my plans

Lord, I want to discuss with You my plans, dreams, and my pursuits. I never tire of telling You these things. I need the renewal of Your approval, the repetition of Your consent, my Father and Creator.

I want to do so much, Lord. I want to be creative in my life. I want to have success in something serious, great, and wonderful.

I fervently desire that in my brief passing in this world I will leave a mark, to have influence on my fellow man.

God, perhaps this is selfishness? Is this prayer a sin?

God, no! I don't believe it. Not because I am free of the pride so despised by You. Not at all. But because I firmly believe that You won't allow me not to arrange plans.

You don't want Your creation, humankind or any human being to pass away from the earth without leaving traces, without realizing something important and great. You didn't create us for small things.

You planted in me the yearning for creativity. You made my imagination soar, so that it is in a place that it may envision and design things.

I would be a traitor to You if I should not desire and if I should not work hard in order to achieve something worthwhile in my lifetime.

But whatever I ask for, Jesus, I don't do it out of the empty and blind exaggeration of my ego, which isn't even worthy of Your disdain. Like a human being, like one of Your sons, I feel that I must honor You.

Tomorrow, if I accomplish something, Lord, by Your aid, it won't interest me in the least for people to hear my name. It is enough if they can say: "A man, a child of God, did this fine deed."

I want my life's work to be ascribed to Your glory, to the honor of Your creation of mankind. Therefore I don't have the right to imagine it a small matter. In this instance I can't be frugal.

In such matters, Lord, I feel frugality to be a sin.

O Jesus Christ, bless my plans.

Remove every element of sinfulness from my dreams.

Sanctify my intentions.

Make my visions a tangible reality.

16

I have been hit by failure

I am afflicted, God. My failure today plunged a knife into my heart.

I started out with so many hopes. I was well prepared. I had absolute certainty of my success.

But I was wrong. One disaster after another led me into misfortune that cost me dearly, because I didn't expect it.

I am suffering.

I feel hopeless.

I feel tired.

My will went numb. How can I try to make another attempt?

I look for refuge in You. Comfort me, my Christ.

Give me courage to act.

Teach me to be patient.

Grant me the wisdom and the patience that are necessary to study my failure and objectively and maturely to determine the reasons why it happened so that I can overcome it easier.

Disperse the clouds of pessimism, my Father, that hang on me as heavy as a lead weight.

Give me the eagerness to work again.

Renew my decisiveness that was shocked and hurt by my failure. Turn its poisonous stinger from an occasion for grief into an incentive for work and creativity.

Let today be the basis for a new jump forward. Let it be a starting point, God, for a path to victory. Make my failure a passageway through which I will more quickly arrive at success. Amen.

17

I am upset, my God

Immortal Comforter, I am again turning to You. You are my refuge. I calm down under Your watch. Your caress quiets the turmoil in my heart.

God, I am upset. Confusion in my feelings has control over me.

Turmoil and excitement.

Yet another time that I am a prisoner of my strong emotions. I am suffering so much.

God, You see what is happening in my vulnerable heart. One day I strongly like this or that person. I am enchanted by them. And the next day maybe I can't stand them at all. From the feeling of love I fall into the feeling of disdain, maybe even into hatred and hostility.

I thirst for love. I want the people to love me in a rather exclusive way. But this becomes an upsetting thing, God. When I think or perceive that the other person doesn't care for me, I feel hurt. At that very same moment a storm breaks out within me that wounds my heart.

O my Christ, command the storm to subside. Give me tranquility. Let Your peace enter my heart and expel the bustle of turmoil.

Grant me the grand gift of self-control over my emotions. Make me my heart's navigator, or better yet, You take the wheel Yourself.

Dispel my excitement. Lessen the explosiveness of certain definite conditions.

Lower the temperature that turns my soul into a volcano.

I beg for peace.

I plead for tranquility.

Lord, with open arms I await Your arrival. Don't delay, Unique Peacemaker.

18

Release me from weariness

Have pity on me, O Lord, take a look at my labor and hard work. My life is tough.

I am very tired, O Christ. Fatigue has set into every fiber of my body. The day has not progressed far and already I am possessed by weariness. A feeling of inertia runs through my blood.

I feel tired, like I am slowly dying. Its poison drips slowly drop by drop into my body.

It is killing me little by little.

How should I be so tired at the beginning of my life! God, isn't it a pity, a sin? It can't be possible that You brought me to life just for this.

Deliver me, then, O Jesus, from the oppression of fatigue.

You said, *"Come to me, all you who are weary and heavy burdened, and I will give you rest."*[19] Behold, we come to You, we recline upon Your chest exhausted. Perhaps we may fall asleep at Your feet.

What a happiness if we would be able to fall asleep calm and cheerful in Your embrace, like a child in its mother's arms! What happiness if we would arise refreshed, rested, fresh, ready to make a start, ready to conquer life!

Give me rest, Lord.

Grant my heart ease and relaxation.

Coordinate the conditions in my life, so that my body and my tired being are able to breathe again, and to escape from the constant stress. Let my mind be free from over exhaustion.

You and only You have the ability to give us rest. Only You can breathe new life, eagerness, and endurance into our minds, hands, legs, and eyes. Your breathe has the capability to refresh, to invigorate, and to equip a person with new strength, zest, and moving force.

The expectation for Your intervention, the certainty that You would not be late, already makes my tiredness more bearable. Fatigue's heavy cloudiness has already begun to thin out.

Thank you, Lord.

19

Everyone is waiting for You

Our Father, who art in heaven …Thy Kingdom come….[20] We ask that Your Kingdom come. We have lived long enough in hell.

How long, Lord, will You allow Satan to conduct as a maestro the symphony of corruption and death on the earth?

For how long will the stench of decay choke the sweet smell of the lilies?

For how long will the most treacherous plans be hidden behind smiles?

For how long will human beings pursue the love of the night and yearn for the dark?

Great Expected Lord, there is already enough of the kingdom of lies and injustice. There is enough of the rule of corruption and hunger. *Thy Kingdom come.*[21]

May the Kingdom of Thy Love come. This ought to be the law we live by, and let it be a substitute for the law of evil that governs us.

May the Kingdom of Thy Righteousness come, of Thy Faithfulness, of Thy Holiness, of Thy Truth.

It's already time for You to reign. In our hearts. In our homes. In our cities. In our schools. In our scientific laboratories. And in our factories and fields.

A million hands are raised in an act of petition to You, O King. A million eyes implore You. Their desire for these things dries their tears.

Come, O Heavenly King, and take over.

The world is Yours.

Take on the power and authority.

O how blessed an overthrow of the old conditions! Your authority won't have anything that reminds us of the ordinary meaning of this word. Your authority won't have any relationship to any earthly authority.

May Your Kingdom come to my soul. Become the holy Lord of my will, my words, and my actions.

I hand my heart over to You. Modern idols have sufficiently taken advantage of my heart. Various tyrants have sufficiently lorded over it. It is now time for You God, to take over.

Our expectation has no further margins. The world is waiting for You.

For Yours is the Kingdom, and the power and the glory, now and forever and unto the ages of ages. Amen.[22]

20

The happiness of being able to speak

How can I describe the happiness of being able to speak, O Word of God? To be able to formulate my thoughts constantly, express my feelings, and make my impressions evident. To be able to come into contact with my brethren and with You.

How would I be if I were unable to read and write? My heartfelt gratitude gushes forth from my soul.

I feel guilty before Your presence, though, Lord. I don't use the gift of speech that You graced me with in either a holy or responsible way.

How many puffs of hot air are wasted every day, and how much meaningless chatter! How many times I have made my tongue a weapon for committing injustice and telling lies!

Don't condemn me, please, for the sinful and incomprehensible use of this extremely valuable gift. But help me.

Sanctify and correct my tongue's performance in my life so that from my mouth will come out only *whatever is true, whatever is just, whatever is pure, whatever is dear, whatever is gracious....*[23]

Don't let me hurt other people by my words. Don't let my speech and my everyday behavior create wounds.

Don't let me dip my tongue or my pen into mud. I wish that whatever I may say would be able to stand the light, to have a crystal-clear transparency, and not to be afraid of publicity.

May my words become bearers and makers of joy. May they be, God, tasteful and pleasant. May they be words that will console those who suffer, encourage those who are shaken, enliven those who are indecisive and hesitant.

That they could bring a grateful, wholly pure laugh to the mouths of my brethren, a relief, a strengthening relaxation in the stress of work.

God, grant me the gift of discernment, so that I know when to speak, where, and how much. What I should say and how to say it.

Consent to use my poor tongue for the promotion of what is good and just.

Make it an instrument of holiness.

21

I live among human beings

Lord, I live among human beings. Wherever I go, wherever I stand, I find myself with people I know and don't know, good and bad.

I see it, and You see it much better, that other people influence me. Either a little or a lot I feel them burden my soul, Invisible Lord, and leave their traces on my personality, acting more or less formatively on my character.

Their ideas either embrace mine or push them away.

Their habits are grafted onto my life.

Their ideals, integrity, and cynicism leave something or take something from my heart.

I see that I'm a sensitive recipient. The presence of other people comprises a mighty factor in my life. So I find refuge in You and I ask for assistance.

Give me, God, right judgment and perception to discern good from bad influences.

Give me wisdom to know who does me good, who helps me in lifting my spirit and who influences me badly and provokes corruption in my ethical make up.

Bestow on me the power, God, that I may distance myself from the direct influence of those people who affect me so that I do bad things, even though I might have had ties to them just yesterday.

And wherever cooperation and contact with them are inevitable, O Almighty Savior, erect a protective net all around me. In it may the biggest if not the entire amount of the bad influence from these other people be caught.

Build up my soul to be strong and enduring, diminish my soft attitude toward evil, negative influences.

Put bright people beside me. Give me the grace to discover them. Their presence is so indispensable to me.

The radiance of their gracious personalities is what my soul needs.

O God-man, increase Your influence over me.

Don't let other hands shape my heart.

Don't let barbaric, wicked feet tread the inner temple of my heart.

22

My soul thirsts for the Living God

Unfathomable, Incomprehensible, Eternal God, the desire burns in me to get to know You. Beyond the thirst for knowledge that holds science as its objective, it tortures me with a sweet torment, the longing for Your knowledge. *My soul thirsts for the living God.*[24]

O that I could reach You!

That my spirit might be immersed in Your eternity to face Your light. I raise a thousand hands to touch You. With wide open, dilated eyes I am searching for Your face.

My entire being was transformed into an arrow, shearing the heavens to pursue You.

All of the pores of my existence are open to You, that they might receive any one of Your messages or sign of Your presence.

When will You speak?

When will You reveal Yourself?

When will Your knowledge, against which all other knowledge is like a lamentable, tattered rag, dwell in me at last?

I thirst for You, my Known Unknown.

Demolish the wall the world has erected around me that doesn't let me see You.

Remove the impenetrable cover of the passions that hide the blessed sight of You.

Cleanse my heart of all impurity.

You said: *Blessed are the pure in heart, for they will see God.*[25]

Wash my spirit.

Loosen Your silence.

Reveal Your true face to me, even for a moment. I am so nostalgic of You.

Nothing can satisfy me except for You.

My God, respond to my supplication. Make me worthy of Your acquaintance.

I would love You then so much more. And I would seek You with greater passion.

23

Save me from laziness

My God, a lazy attitude often captivates me. Something that is both sloth and laziness is establishing itself within my being. I get a heavy feeling and don't have the appetite for sober, intense work.

I'm suffering, God, because of this issue. I see that I waste time. Days go by. A mass of work that intimidates me piles up.

My heart becomes an untended field open to any intrusion. The most sinful things pass back and forth in my soul, and I have neither the appetite nor the disposition to resist them.

My God, save me from this indolence which is holding me in its soft hands at this very moment.

Expel the sweet sleepiness from my limbs.
Shake the drowsiness from my eyelids.
Give me wakefulness, O Untired Vigilant.
Fortify me to watch over myself and hurl myself into work and toilsome jobs.

Arm my soul with vigilance. Let me hear even in the depths of my being the echo of Your commandment, *Be watchful in all things.*[26]

Please, God, give me wakefulness, appetite to do work, and a proper attitude *to fight the good fight.*[27]

24

The three agents

Tonight, my Maker, I'm going to tell You again about the ruthless problem that I just faced. About the relationship between three factors: me, the others, and God.

That these three factors have to find their respective places harmoniously in my life is wholly obvious to me.

But, God, it is so hard! Until a little while ago, I wouldn't even have thought of the question. I was ignorant that it was a problem.

You, God, I essentially did not give thought to. You know. I did not even pray. I marginalized the factor "God" in my life.

The factor "me" suffered from overdevelopment, from a kind of spiritual obesity.

And the factor "others" I would leave to play an odd role in my life's progress. At one time, God, I used to hold others in high esteem, at another time I would hold the same people in scorn. So often I felt like I loved them, and other times I fall to having an unheard-of indifference, into coldness in their presence, that even I myself couldn't explain it.

It's obvious, God, that these three factors weren't at all well situated in my life. And they continue not to be.

That's why I feel this restlessness. I am in suspense. I feel that I'm missing a spiritual and ethical balance. I want to find the most concise way of reaching a solution for my problem.

Help me to place properly in my life the three vital agents: You, the others, myself.

Restore the harmony.

Let me learn to see You as my Father, Omnipotent, Omniscient, Eternal and Absolute, the Origin and End of all.

Instruct my heart to see others as my brothers and sisters, as Your children.

Enlighten me to comprehend that I have no reason to exist other than You. That my mission in this world is to liken myself to You and serve my brothers and sisters.

Make all these things the blood in my heart, the life that exists in every last cell in my body.

Resolve, Lord, my problem.

25

Save me from the temptations

Save me, Lord. Temptations have surrounded me. They fling themselves rabidly at me from outside of me. They hammer at me from within.

I am living under unbearable stress.

My blood boils.

The excitement has an effect on even the smallest muscle in my body. Empower me, Father, not to yield to this uprising of my body. Don't let me compromise with the sub-human that attacks me.

Compromise in this case is death.

God, make me irreconcilable, harsh, formidable and unyielding in the battle against temptations.

Change my body into steel, and my fleshy heart into granite.

O God, how difficult this struggle is! It stops my breath. My prayer becomes screaming.

Save me.

Become my protector at this difficult hour.

Don't delay, God! You want me to remain upright and blameless. You want me to be free and pure. You were crucified, my Jesus, so that I might overcome sin, to slay the monster that nests in my heart. Certainly You won't leave me. *God, attend to my assistance, hurry to my aid.*[28]

Please I pray to You, Omnipotent God, order the storm to subside.

Cool my hot face with the breeze of Your grace.

Enable my will that struggles desperately to escape the smothering embrace of evil.

Let loose the rain of Your love, so that it extinguishes the fires of the passions. Hold me upright. Grant me victory.

Keep my face clean, Lord.

Deliver me, Lord, from this moment of anxiety and gracelessness.

26

The hunger for happiness tortures me

O Jesus Christ, the hunger for happiness tortures me. My prayer is a request for joy.

Until now, Lord, I had hurt so much. Oh! My days were gray and obscure up to now. Sorrow, You know, became my lonesome shadow.

My home always had its share of deaths, deprivation, and calamities.

Under the pressure of grief, Jesus, I was looking so many times for happiness on easy roads. You were watching me. Small handy joys that modern life offers became welcome to me. I was tied to cheap, sinful joys.

But You know, God, that I always remained hungry. My heart would never eat to its content.

Days and months of affliction devoured the seconds of happiness and relaxation. Bitterness was the only taste my mouth knew.

God, I hunger for happiness. Don't You pity me?

Give me the manna of Your gladness. Your joy is so great that even the heavens cannot contain it. And Your love will tolerate the fact that I will remain hungry and unhappy?

Truly, I'm not to blame, if I passionately desire and look for happiness. You planted that desire in me. You made my hunger so intense. You made my arms extend so that I might grasp happiness. God, You made my eyes search for it everywhere.

Jesus, You promised us Your joy. *So that they may have my joy fulfilled in them.*[29] Now will You deny that?

If I need to do something to acquire it, show me what it is. Lead me in the way that I might make it take effect.

Your gladness exists in our world, help me recognize it, Lord, from among its imitations.

My God, Lord of blessed joy, grant me a little bit of this joy.

A single droplet of Your joy is equal to an ocean of human happiness.

Drip a little bit of this on my dry lips, O You who are both God and man.

27

Deliver me from selfishness

I praise You for Your love, Father of mercy. I bless You for Your mercy and Your longsuffering. For Your inexhaustible tolerance that I contemplate in Your attitude toward me.

How much can You tolerate me! How You bear my terrible behavior, my monstrous selfishness, O Absolutely All-pure Spirit.

Look! Even today my time was full of selfishness. The center of my life, my dearest enemy, myself.

Forgive me, Lord, for my steady sinfulness. Have mercy on me.

Save me from myself. Crack this tough shell in which my ego has enclosed my being.

How often even today I haven't sought to become the center of everyone else's interests! What I haven't contrived, Lord, to draw attention, to attract admiration, and rather without seeming to make any special effort to do this. And for as many times as I succeeded, what pleasure I didn't taste.

Forgive me, Lord. My God, I was confronted with a heap of serious problems today. I saw pain on many of my colleagues' and fellow workers' faces. However, I passed by essentially indifferent. Because as always there was but one center that magnetically drew my eyesight: my ego. An immovable axle that I constantly revolve around. At whatever point I was, I looked only at myself. My selfish projection was my permanent concern.

When, O Crucified Lord, will I finally surpass this miserable ego? When can my real, true essence be freed from my egotistical bonds?

Jesus, will Your godly example inspire me and Your Cross speak truly to my soul?

My God, My God, deliver me from selfishness, save me from its bonds.

28

Stay with me

My Jesus, stay by me. This night emphasizes the need for Your presence.

Shelter me under Your wings.

Warm my hands within Yours, pierced by nails, but for that reason all the more precious and loved.

Don't leave. Where will You go at this time of the night, Jesus? The night is advancing.

Is there someone who needs You more than me?

People who know me think of me as a calm person, decisive, successful, and well-situated in life. But You know me, Jesus, that deep down I remain a child.

A scared child who feels so uncomfortable in the endless world.

A child who feels lonely and like a stranger, even when other people's love surrounds him.

You are my friend, brother, and Father. Only when I hear the beating of Your heart, do I feel my own calm down.

Near You I breathe in brotherhood, and I overcome my solitude.

Stay a while longer, my Redeemer. Don't be in a hurry to leave. My sinfulness is kicking You out, but Your boundless love is keeping You here.

Oh! Stay with me.

Tell me what I have to do, to hold You here, though it might be only a little while.

One minute near You equals an eternity. In Your presence time stops. It vanishes.

In Your companionship I taste eternal joy.

Stay by me forever, O Jesus.

Third Cycle

*And they fell on their faces
before the throne and
they worshipped God saying:
Amen! Blessing and Glory and Wisdom
and Thanksgiving and Honor
and Power and Might
be to our God,
unto the ages of ages.
Amen.*

Revelation of John 7:11-12

29

I give glory to You

Lord, at Your feet my spirit humbly kneels. I am overflowing with an inexpressible sensation, with a full life, that culminates in a psalm of glorification.

I adore You, I glorify You, Eternal and Great Maker of beauty and power.

How much beauty You spread out before my eyes this very morning! No matter how much you might hide Yourself and try to remain unseen, I still see You.

I see You, God, behind the Sun that rises again refreshed and lifelike and spreads warm, bright fingers over the earth.

I see You in the calm, transparent morning mist that floats over the trees.

I see You in the night that leaves discreetly, after it granted me the rest and the rejuvenation of my powers through a deep and calm sleep.

I follow the calm rising of creation, the life that awakens, the dewy start of a new day.

Everything bears expressions of this. They denote Your presence. They announce Your wisdom and Your tender affection.

Among Your *creatures* and the *works of Your hands* I recognize and *I perceive* this morning *Your perpetual power and divinity.*[30]

I see and I am vibrant with an inner composure for Your glorification. But my earthly mouth is unable to transform the waves of my adoring sensations into waves of speech.

Read, O Lord, my morning doxology in my heart.

Hear my hymns to Your glory that echo back and forth in my breast.

30

I praise You for the light

Glory to You, Lord, who shows light. O *Father of lights*, let me sing hymns to You about the light that encircles me, that showers me at this midday hour, by the sea, under Your Sun.

Waterfalls of light, sent down by Your hands, slip along the blue infinity of water. They knead the Sun into the sea, they make every drop of water into Sun, they give birth to a million Suns.

The sand, Lord, is transformed into pure white snow. Its poor insignificant grains become diamonds that sparkle with thousands of light beams.

So much light! White, warm, spotless.

I feel like I'm swimming in an ocean of light. I feel like I'm swimming in the Sun.

God, what happiness, O God! What an exaltation of life!

I wish the world would stop in such a moment like this when all is light.

O Fashioner of Light, Creator of the Sun, I give You thanks, I praise You for the rivers of light that undulate in front of my awe-struck eyes.

I glorify You also for these eyes that You graced me with, so that I can rejoice in such a wholly bright, all-white beauty.

31

You were crucified for me

O my Jesus, You were crucified for me.

O my Jesus, You were crucified for me.

How should I tell You what I feel, when I meditate on this event? How can I express in words of prayer the flood that inundates my internal space when I raise my eyes to Your Cross?

For me! What am I? An insignificant person. *I am dirt and ashes.*[31] Someone who has lost his humanity.

A nothing, who hardly has any value for anyone to consider.

But, my Savior, for this nothing, You were nailed on the wood of the Cross.

For me nails were driven through Your hands.

For me, Your feet were nailed.

Oh! I'm not worthy of this.

For me they gave You gall and vinegar to drink.

How can I endure the sight of beholding You, who were *comely in beauty beside the sons of men,*[32] hanged naked, condemned, covered with blood?

Oh! I am not worthy of this.

I am not worthy of this.

My mind comes to a stop when I consider that the most terrifying tragedy in the world happened for me, living in a home like millions of other homes. My Jesus, I am entirely sinful. But also entirely thankful.

Your sacrifice for my sake can't be measured by any means.

I thank You my Redeemer and my Savior, and my Crucified Lord. I am at a loss for words. I can't speak. It is profane for me to enclose within the stifling boundaries of the words my inexpressible feelings.

Kneeling before Your Cross, I am weeping and full of gratitude.

32

Prayer for the beginning of a new day

Lord, I thank You for the night that just passed. The new day is outside of my open window. Once I wake up I want my first words and my first thoughts to be about You, my Father and Maker.

I glorify You along with the birds who sing on the pine tree in our yard.

I sing hymns along with the poplars next to the stream across the way, that shake their straight trunks up high while their leaves shiver in the effort.

I praise You together with the morning breeze that cools my face, driving away the last remnant of sleep from my limbs.

I let my words of glorification be woven together with the song of the water that echoes cheerfully in the stream.

I'd like my prayer, God, to go up to Your Throne like the sweet scent of flowers and to be as clean as the drops of dew that lightly hang on the leaves' edges.

The creation speaks in so many ways about You!

It is so good for me to speculate on this morning beauty and to raise my soul up to You.

May You be glorified, O God.

33

We bless You because we can think

I think of You tonight full of awe, awe and gratitude, Boundless, Ineffable, Transcendent God. Who are above all material substance. It isn't the night that contributes to this. It is the contact with human thought, with the spirit, which You implanted in the depths of our being.

A little while ago I finished reading a book. How extraordinary it was, God! Every time I follow in some significant text the development of some important thought, the brilliance of a powerful spirit, I am completely overcome by awe and thankfulness.

You made us "thinking beings," "thinking reeds," as a child of Yours once stated. An unspoken, indescribable fact. The gift that we could think, compose or analyze.

To fly on wings of thought, to walk in the meadows of the spirit.

We glorify You, Only Wise Lord, because You gave us the faculty of thought, the ability to approach wisdom.

We sing hymns to You because we can write books and build scientific knowledge.

Heavy scientific writings are hymns to Your name, O All Wise, even though they may not deal directly with You. From their thickly printed pages that treat issues of physics, chemistry, law, or linguistics, emanates the hymn of the human spirit sent toward Your Eternal Spirit.

And if our own spirit might be constantly able to present these kinds of achievements, what should we think about You, the mind who is above the world and above heaven, the inexhaustible source of wisdom.

Our prayer tonight is comprised of a dizzying joy, awe, and thanksgiving.

34

I thank You because I am alive

My God, I thank You because I am a living being. I thank You because I can feel my blood running warm in me. Because I can see, rejoice, think, plan, dream, love, and work.

You could have left me in a state of not being, in absolute nothingness. I try to comprehend how I would have been then. A totally unsuccessful attempt. The concept of non-being, of perfect nothingness, brings me to a bottomless abyss, to something dark and terrible.

You saved me, You who are the Beginningless and Immortal Life.

You granted me life.

And together with life You gave me so many other gifts, so that I could live better and more deeply.

Lord, You are the Life.

You are the perfect, absolute, extremely beautiful Life, that the suspicion or fear of death doesn't obscure and the presence of evil doesn't mar.

I know that our own lives have their source in You. *You are He who gives life, breath, and all things.*[33]

What else should we say to You except a sincere "Thank You"? How can we worthily glorify You?

O Imperishable Creator, make us live every day even more in an authentic and true life.

Transform our lives and lift them more and more from the biological and physical level to the spiritual and supernatural plane.

Transfuse in us the juices and waters of life, *for from You is the Source of Life.*[34]

35

The Hosanna of my freedom

Father, a shudder of deep and unspeakable joy passes through me tonight. I feel the huge value You gave to us as human beings by endowing us with freedom, a freedom that constitutes the special characteristic of Your Divine Being.

God, sometimes this gift of Yours seemed a heavy and harsh lot for me. How much pain I felt, that I was obligated to pick between two or more solutions at various difficult times in my life. Then freedom seemed unbearably painful, God.

Doubtlessly these were times of weakness.

But this evening the sense of my freedom brings a sacred intoxication. It defines me as a human being, it gives me wings, it lifts me up.

We offer hymns to You, Father and Liberator. We deposit our "Hosanna" to Your love, because You blew the breath of freedom into cold, lifeless chests, because You kneaded us with it, because You placed us inside the freedom, like eagles on the sky-blue heights.

I tremble when I think how much our freedom cost Your heart.

The entire mystery of Your divine pain is hidden behind our freedom. This freedom cost You the Incarnation, the Martyrdom, and the Crucifixion of Your Son.

Jesus had to be crucified, Jesus had to suffer, to be imprisoned in a tomb, to rise from the dead, so that I can freely breathe. We remember, Lord, what You said to us: *If the Son makes you free you will be free indeed.*[35]

God's blood had to be shed, so that our lost freedom be regained.

O my Free Liberator! Tonight I deposit at Your throne, beside the heaps of my old broken chain of bondage, the "Hosanna" of my freedom.

36

I see You in the midst of the storm

Omnipotent Lord, how great and mighty You revealed Yourself in the midst of the storm that broke out a little while ago.

I hear You in the roar of the waves, I detect You beneath the huge mass of the water that covers the rocks of the coastline with froth.

I see Your divine hand that provokes the sea's uneasiness.

Your power wanders behind the foamy wave-crests, it emerges beside the everlasting rocks of the seashore.

I glorify You, Lord.

In the half-darkness, I see the trees bending under the wind's impetus. I see the lightning tear the sky in a blinding slice. I hear the rain beating on the rooftops, and scratch at the road's surface.

I hear You in the violent wind.

I uncover You in the rain's rhythm.

I hear You in the echo of the thunder.

The storm sings hymns to Your infinite power, God.

The rainstorm builds Your Majesty.

And the dark and stormy sea announces Your colossal, infinite might.

On my knees, small and weak I lift up my hands to You, I raise my heart to sing to You about Your great glory and about Your immeasurable power.

37

I thank You for the silence

You came so silently, that I didn't notice You, Lord. And I wouldn't have realized that You are here if a state of tranquility hadn't enveloped me. Very few times I have experienced such a calm night.

Every noise dissolved into the darkness. Every voice has been extinguished. I can't get enough of hearing the silence. Everything is mute. Breaths are halted.

In the silence I feel You near me, my Adorable Lord, Creator of tranquility.

I glorify You because of this extraordinary creation of Yours that is called silence. I give You thanks for the absence of every sound this evening.

The hour is spent. But the hint of sleepiness doesn't come across me.

You are beside me and that's enough. God, Ocean of tranquility, You see my soul in a state of glorifying You. You see my heart that is grateful to You for this quietness.

When, Lord, I collect myself to go to sleep in a little while, You will stay tenderly beside my pillow. Because of this my sleep will be peaceful and won't stir up nightmares.

O You, who have the power to create a silence that is more eloquent than our vain human babbling and our nerve-wracking noises, send me such calm and quiet nights more often.

38

You have shown me a true human being

My God, I complained so often to You. I told You about how there are less and less true people in our days.

I protested because sin gallops along our asphalt paved roads under neon signs.

Again almost desperately I spoke the words of Your prophet: *Everyone was turning away, and at the same time were rendered useless, there is not a person who is upright, there is not even one.*[36]

I was waiting for Your answer, Lord.

You know that I was very much pressured by feelings of pessimism.

But today, though, You spoke to me.

You showed me a person. I recovered my breath. My soul was relieved.

He was one of Your own. Showered with goodness and truth. An upright person, clear as crystal, full of grace. A transmitter of life.

He didn't say at all the word "God" in our conversation. But for me it cannot be disputed that he was one of Your chosen ones, a citizen of Your Kingdom.

It did me so much good that You sent him in my path today. Thank You. It was absolutely necessary for me.

A strong antidote for the poison of my disenchantment that pours over me when I think deeply about our society.

I thank You for this true human being.

I magnify You, Lord, because from the filth of our corruption You can fashion true Christians and authentic people. When we see them, we draw upon new courage. They are heralds of Your existence, of Your love.

Whatever is beautiful at this moment on this earth, they are.

Bring them together. Multiply them.

Today, right now, we have an absolutely urgent need for them, Lord.

39

You filled our neighborhoods with children

Heavenly Father, a portion of our world still exists that reminds us of Eden. Children.

What a precious element for our lives, my God, are the little children! What eloquent witnesses of Your presence!

In their eyes, where memories of scenes of bloodshed do not darken and the fever of the passions doesn't burn, Your holiness is reflected.

In their movements full of trust and simplicity, the need for our return to simplicity and for putting aside the masks we often wear is intensely accentuated.

And in their carefree and innocent singing, in their crystal-clear laughter without a hint of cloudiness, we discover Your love, a love that reminds us that You are with us. You take daily care of us much more than earthly fathers for their children.

We bless You, Lord, because You filled neighborhoods with children.

We thank You, because You let our dark, distracted gaze encounter the surprised, pure gaze of the little children.

We sing hymns to You because You gave the children's laughter the power to get rid of our frowns, to bring us a breath of sanctity, a breeze of Paradise.

O that You had made us like children again! That You would help us to turn, and become *as children*.[37]

Fourth Cycle

First of all then,
I ask that supplications, prayers,
intercessions and thanksgivings
be made for all men.

I Timothy 2:1

40

I pray to You on behalf of our world

Lord, I pray to You about our world. I pray to You about our universe.

God, tonight my heart widens. Its bounds are removed, its circle enlarges. I see an ocean of people through the help of its imagination that You gave me.

People of every country, of every land. Everyone and all are my contemporary. They live in the very same moment that I live. White, black, yellow, red-skinned, billions of souls. They are my brothers and sisters. Your children.

It is so good for me, my God, to consider that our world is full of people, that I am not the only inhabitant of Earth.

I pray to You, Jesus, for all my brothers and sisters of the entire world. I feel united with them around You as the center. I feel the vibrations of the joy of the spiritual international family that has You as the center.

Let Your light, Lord, come to all hearts. Up there in the frozen lands of ice, down in sun-scorched Africa, over in the Far East.

All the people who live today on earth come to know You. All those who inhabit large cities, all those who live in the tiniest villages lost in dense forests or on far off islands.

Let Your Sun rise even in those places where law doesn't exist, or in places of exile, or in the depths of mines.

Stoop down to our world. Don't turn Your face away from our planet.

It is Yours.

Do not allow the cry of our injustice and lawlessness prevent You from hearing the sobbing for our decadence. You see the yearning of the people, Your children, for something new.

May Your Kingdom come to our Earth. You, Beginningless Creator, who gave us the ability to fly away from the Earth, and to other stars, don't forget man's first abode.

Beautify our lives on Earth.

Sanctify them.

God, I pray to You on behalf of our world. For my brothers and sisters of the entire world.

41

Make our work pleasant

God, at dawn, as I hear people going to their jobs, I consider again the same problem: their work.

For so many millions of souls, work is a pain, a disappointment, and a weight that can't be lifted. For innumerable people, my God, work has become a tragedy if not a crime or a curse.

Today I want to dedicate my prayer to this question, which I feel pressing on me.

Please, Lord, don't leave this problem unresolved. Grant that better conditions hold up on this day in all the factories, offices, shops, and all portions of human activity.

Make cooperation among colleagues a pleasant reality.

Make the cooperation between employer and employee a source of joy and blessed productivity, and not a cause for hate, intrigue, or injustice.

God, at least today, don't allow the hours people work to go beyond the ability of people to bear.

Don't let labor break the laborers. Don't let the mind, body, nerves, eyes, hands, or feet build up so much trouble and worry that sleep won't be able to get rid of.

Lord, make it so that the mass of labor that millions of people produce today will not be a contributing factor to evil, but to prosperity.

And in the evening, God, when we return to our homes after work, let us be deeply satisfied. Let not the pain of injustice press the heart. Let the heart be filled with the joy of a productive day, a just compensation and a work satisfying our desire for creativity.

Lord, make each of us worthy today to be a contributor to raising the quality of the conditions in our working environment.

42

Prayer for the families of our neighborhoods

My God, I can't be quiet. My mind wanders around and enters the many different houses of our neighborhood that do not live in peace.

The evening is very calm. But hearts are agitated and sunken in anxiety. The day has drawn to its close, Father, but the problems that besiege many families remain open. The eyes become burdened with obscure shadows and the hearts are heavy.

I pray to You, God, for the families of my neighborhood. Visit them.

Throw their troubles out of them and bring hope. Make the daily cares that devour the heart disappear.

Present solutions to life's problems.

Settle the disturbed relationships among members of different families whom I know or I don't know.

O Lord, remind the people of our area that You exist, that You are a strong and loving Protector. How much they will be relieved when they've heard still another time Jesus' words:

Look at the birds of the sky, how they neither sow nor reap nor gather crops into storehouses, and our Father in heaven feeds them. Are you not rather different from them?[38]

Keep away, Lord, anything that causes the disappearance of peace from our souls and the escape of sleep from our eyes.

Stay a little while more tonight in our neighborhood.

Spread peace along with the night. Let the harshness of the day and its struggles not spread also over the night, God.

43

Prayer for my parents

My Heavenly Father, I pray to You for my father and my mother. I am both Your child and theirs. I want to unite them to You in an arc of prayer. Thus we should stay united in life forever and in death and in eternity as parents and children.

Open Your arms and cover them with blessings. Sow happiness in their hearts.

God, don't let them know dark or bitter days.

Multiply the years of their lives and make them years of peace and rejoicing. *In glory and honor crown them.*[39]

Don't let it happen, Lord, that we, their children, cause any bitterness to them.

Make our lives perfect, so that it will be a source of happiness and deep satisfaction for them.

My Heavenly Father, I fervently pray to You for my father and my mother.

44

Prayer for my teachers

All Wise and Holy God, I pray to You for my teachers and instructors. For all the people who have offered the dew of knowledge to my thirsty intellect.

I pray to You for all those who taught me to read and write. For all those who are conducting me into the world of science and knowledge.

Supply them with forbearance, with health, and with patience. Offer them the satisfaction of seeing their students' progress in every sector of their studies.

Give, Lord, my instructors light from Your light. Wisdom from the ocean of Your wisdom. Happiness from Your blessedness.

May Your Spirit cover their spirits. Let Your Spirit find rest in their hearts. Amen.

45

Forgive those who hurt me

Forgive them, Lord. Forgive those people who did wrong to me, who were unfair to me, and hurt me. This is so difficult to say these words, God. I try hard still to suppress the anger that boils within me. My hurt and indignation were unbearable. Because the blow they caused me was painful.

You saw it, Christ.

I thank You because You helped me control myself.

In the condition I was, I could have done much wrong. I went through critical hours.

Thank You for guarding me against the destructive counselor which is called vindictiveness.

Lord, please forgive them. Remembering Your being nailed, on the Cross, I am calming down and filling up with the ability to say again: Forgive my enemies. Those who behaved even worse than enemies to me.

Enlighten them to understand that they were wrong, and that they have committed a sin.

Reveal the truth to them.

Remove the blinds of hate that blind them and won't let them see.

God, guard them by Your love, so that nothing bad may happen to them.

Provide them with the ability not to proceed again with actions like today's which likely created irreparable damage.

Lord, bless those who injured me.

Let Your grace, Your enlightenment, and Your mercy, shelter their souls.

46

Prayer for the sick

God, what beauty! An extraordinary morning! My glorification of You, like a flood that can't be restrained rises within me.

I give thanks for the dawn, for the day that has just begun.

I give thanks for the life that vibrates in my being.

What a great feeling to be alive, to walk, to run!

But, Lord, I think at this moment about the many people who right now, like yesterday and the day before, will remain bed-ridden. My thought rushes to the hospitals, the asylums, and the homes that contain sick people. To those who, with unspeakable sorrow, will follow the course of the Sun in its rising, reaching midheaven, and set while they are staying in the same position, immovable, God, *upon the bed of their grief.*[40]

O my Christ, I can't do anything else for them except pray.

Please, Jesus, make their illnesses less painful. Reduce the intensity and extent of their pains.

For a person made to be alive, Lord, to be glad, to go around from place to place, to work creatively, it is too much that he or she remain for days, months, or even years in bed. Don't add suffering to this.

Please intervene, Physician of bodies and souls, so that every surgery that happens today will be successful.

Please enlighten the doctors so that they proceed with the correct diagnoses.

Lord, make more effective the medications that will be used.

Grant patience and a better disposition unto the sick that they accept more easily the difficult and painful remedies and interventions.

God, promote resolutely our research and struggle to fight against certain diseases that flog our world like lashes.

Grant healing to the millions of sick.

To the sick people of our cities, of our countries, and of the whole world, let more mercy be upon them, O Jesus.

Pick them up in the fastest possible way, stand them upright and strong on the ground, ready to live, work, and rejoice with us. Amen.

Prayer for my fellow students

Ocean of Wisdom, Father of Light, I glorify You because You opened the road to knowledge and education for me.

I thank You because You made me a student and situated me among a crowd of other young people who toil to conquer over science.

For all these people I want to pray to You now. For my fellow students.

Wrap us, God, in Your love. The thing which would unite us should be love without dark spots, without hidden agendas or selfish motives.

A bond that is not hypocritical should bind us together unbroken within the classrooms, the amphitheaters and the courtyards of our schools.

Christ, don't let malice and selfish competition develop between us, between fellow students.

Throw envy and the variety of enmities far away from us.

God, let us not see each other like future professional rivals, but colleagues and co-workers in a sacred endeavor.

Fill us with enthusiasm for our field of study and with a spirit of diligent conscience for practical work.

To our souls let Your Spirit come, the Spirit of wisdom, the Spirit of prudence, the Spirit of the fear of God, the Spirit of love, the Spirit of power, the Spirit of sanctification, the Spirit of unity, and the Spirit of creativity.

Lord, sanctify the interaction between colleagues of different schools. Raise these relationships to a higher level, where the air is clean and the horizon is open.

Let a new spirit be instituted, Lord. A new order.

We beseech You, let our student world become a different kind of world.

On it let the stamp of Your Spirit be impressed more intensely.

48

Protect us from the idols

God, how could You let this happen? How did You tolerate false idols to be stood up again? Doesn't it *irritate Your Spirit*, the Holy Spirit, when *You see the cities which are given to idols?*[41]

Doesn't it fuel Your sacred anger that our lives became a degenerative idolatry?

Don't You see that the adoration of certain modern idols reaches a status of delirium, and comes close to the boundaries of insanity?

God, monstrous and unnatural images, enchanting and placed on our crossroads!

With the kind of voracious eye, with the mouth that devours never feeling full, with teeth that grind millions of human beings, even tender youth and children.

Oh! It can't be possible!

Lord, free us from idols then. Knock them down. Don't You see them transforming our lives into a fever, hedonism, and boredom?

Free the tender adolescents, save those at the age of their ripening.

Our roads have been filled up with filth, and our houses have been filled up with filth.

It is enough already, my God, don't put Your help too far away.

Sweep the idols away, sweep away death, clog up the flow of debauchery.

You told us, All Good, with Your caring voice: *Children, protect yourself from false images.*[42]

For us, though, it is very hard to guard ourselves. Therefore enlighten us.

Enlighten Your world.

Save us from the false images, from the modern idols, the Beginningless, the Indescribable, the Only True God.

49

Reveal Your truth

You are The Way, the Truth, and the Life.[43] You are a light without shadows, my God, which never goes out, but remains forever lit, unchanging and gladsome.

Jesus, become the way for my errant brothers who wandered off course, for as many people as those who wander in dark labyrinths, in confusion. They are staggering, Lord. They are reeling. They are lost in thousands of turning points with thousands of ways to go. They don't even find one guiding inscription. Reveal Your way to them.

Present Yourself before their astonished eyes, because You, Jesus, are the Way.

Incarnate Truth, reveal the truth to the thousands of our brothers and sisters who choke and faint engulfed by lies. You, with one motion, have the power and the means to lay lies bare and to free the soul from its control.

Make Your Truth obvious, Lord. Establish the Truth in the souls, the eyes, and the lips of the people.

Blow, O God, the breath of life into our beings. Don't You get tired of seeing Your children living a slow death daily?

O my Lord, don't You feel the longing for life that is devouring us?

Don't You feel any sorrow for the dead who circulate on the roads?

We want to live! To live! To live!

Distill life to us from Your life.

Unite us with You unbreakably.

Nourish us with Your living juices.

Lord, enlighten, shed light, give light into our hands, souls, eyes, and onto our roads. Enlighten all those who have not the fortune of knowing You until now.

Just one spark of Your light is enough.

One lightning bolt of Your Holy Spirit is sufficient to bring forth rivers of light, seas of light.

Jesus, *You are The Way, the Truth, and the Life*.[44] You are the *Light of the world*.[45]

I glorify You. I offer my prayer to You.

50

Let hunger be decreased on Earth

So much hunger in the world, Lord, so much hunger. A struggle to get one's bread. A devouring anxiety to get food for the children. Anxiety, and a lack of food.

Hunger for countless people.

God, even tonight many will go to sleep without eating. Without the hope that they'll get their fill tomorrow. Shaking with fear about tomorrow, feeling faint from malnutrition.

As we are able to travel to the Moon, God, is it something tolerable that hunger remains on the Earth?

Is it permissible for feet that tremble from starvation to walk on the same roads that little masterpieces of comfort, speed, and luxury run?

Can men who still crave to get their little bit of bread stand under huge edifices that project phantasmagoric facades toward the Sun?

Lord, I entreat You on behalf of those who hunger. If the rest of us, their brothers, commit the crime of forgetting them, at least You remain their Father.

Oh, let hunger be decreased on Earth.

Jesus, let the curse of starvation disappear from our planet.

You fed more than five thousand with *five loaves and two fishes*.[46] Is it so difficult for You to feed right now our hungry, even if they might number many millions?

Don't leave Your children any longer at our deficient disposition, at the mercy of our cold hearts.

Feed our hungry brothers and sisters, Father.

51

Prayer for those who work under harsh conditions

God, within my room that the Sun bathes, I entertain more painfully the thought that so many people at this same hour work hard in the depths of the earth.

Lowered thousands of meters under the surface of the ground, Lord, in the porticoes and tunnels of the mines, they root out coal and minerals from the bowels of the earth.

The Sun is so far from them. Their eyes don't see green grassy patches or homes or sky or birds. Children's laughter doesn't interrupt the monotony of their hard work, God.

The air they breathe in covers their lungs with a black and sticky mass.

Lord, I pray to You, have pity on these people.

Improve the arrangements of their labor. Equip their health with special endurance. Keep them from the illnesses, above all lung diseases, that threaten them.

Reinforce their faith, Lord, and increase their hope.

May the hours of their rest be more conducive to removing their fatigue and in renewing their strength.

Along with the miners and the coal-miners, I pray on behalf of all our brethren who work in tough jobs, under dangerously health threatening terms.

Don't concede to making the place of their work a place of execution.

Don't let the joy of work be changed into a cry of despair.

Don't let the noise of machines and tools become a funeral march of mourning that lasts for years, for a drawn out daily death of thousands of workers.

God, You have given me especially favorable terms for the performance of my work.

Thank You for that.

But I can't say that I feel no shame when I compare this to the terms of so many of our brethren. Oh, make the differences less.

Show Your good will to the workers who toil under harsh, unbearable conditions.

52

Prayer for those who deny You

Lord, I pray for Your enemies. For the people who deny You. They deny You but they also fight You. What a contradiction, my God, to fight against the One who they say doesn't exist!

They would not speak with such an unquenched passion if they really believed that You do not exist!

Fan the flames of faith in their souls, God, the flames that they wrestle against to cover and extinguish.

Transform them from enemies into people who give You glory, from those who deny You into those who worship You. Let their resistance become devotion to You.

Lord, You know how to enlist Your best Apostles like Saint Paul from among Your enemies. Make something like this happen again in our days, in our places, in our world.

Eternal Ruler of All, I implore You on behalf of everyone else who doesn't believe in You, but who nevertheless don't attack You.

They indifferently shrug their shoulders when someone starts a discussion about You.

They say that You don't exist. They add moreover that for them it is a matter of no consequence whether You exist. They try to certify that Your presence is something completely alien to their lives, something neutral and meaningless.

O Lord, *Show Your face*[47] to them, too.

Let Your silence, which is discreet and full of respect for our freedom, be interrupted from time to time.

Let Your constant, affectionate, limitless intervention be felt sometimes by the eyes too that haven't yet seen You.

Make them overflow, God, with the sensation that You exist.

Thoroughly permeate them with the belief that You are *The God who is the Ruler of All, who was and is and will be.*[48] And that if Your active love, Your holy will, and Your wise power were not here in the world, then everything would have devolved into self-dissolution and annihilation.

My God, my God, make their knees bend and their hearts be lifted up to You.

Their very hearts that declare war on You, deny You, saying they don't know You.

Make their mouths compose the best hymn to Your glory, Eternal Holy God.

53

Prayer for our scientific workplaces and laboratories

Lord, I kneel before Your Majesty. I place a specific request into Your hands: I pray for scientific labs, institutes, and research centers that are scattered all over the world.

Lord, I beg of You, let these workplaces become stations which make Life advance on our planet.

Let a full and true kind of progress spring out from within them, my God, as well as improvement in the structure of things dealing with life, the advancement of science, and the prosperity of all human beings.

Keep giving health and wisdom, God, to those who conduct research. Bring them *wisdom from above, which is pure...peaceful...full of mercy and good fruits.*[49] Distill Your Spirit into them. Let them never lose sight of humankind in their speculations. Don't let them forget that all of the work, discoveries, and inventions have to look out for the good of the people as its end.

Under no circumstances let good will die in the midst of scientific inquiries.

May deep love and respect for humanity always be something that has control over them like an atmosphere of refinement and nobility to places of scientific cultivation.

I yet pray, Lord, don't let these workshops and institutes deteriorate into centers of human arrogance and self-pride that reaches the bounds of hubris.

Let them be Your temples where truly wise men, deeply humble before You, will constantly work to reveal and worship You, *in whom are hidden all of the treasures of wisdom and knowledge.*[50]

54

Let Your love's rain come

We are pitiful, my God. With our own hands we made attempts at wiping out love from our planet.

See, Lord, at how desperately we have diminished love. In the end we achieved, Lord, establishing selfishness and greed as a regulator of our relationships.

Our eyes show the coldness of steel when they do not flash rapaciously or burn with debauchery.

Jesus, O Love beyond all measure, have mercy on us. We are living in conditions that suffocate us.

Show mercy on us, O Love beyond every desire. We are young, at the start of our lives. We can't live without love. Our world is hopelessly strange for us, no matter how much it might enchant us.

How shall we proceed?

Should we kill our own lives, God, in the struggle of self-interests that put us into conflict with one another?

Should we live by contriving methods of extermination? Should we perish in a criminal, illicit competition of treachery and theft?

Let Your love's rain come, Christ, and cleanse our communities from the stain of hate and moisten their closed, water-proof souls.

Let Your love be, let Your love rule everywhere.

We anxiously are waiting the wind of Your tender love to make our shriveled lungs spring to life.

Let this become the Law, the Constitutional Charter of our lives. Make love be our international climate, an atmosphere among all humans.

Bring love, God, to families, cities, villages, and nations.

Evoke a world competition for affection.

Melt the ice that surrounds hearts.

At universities, in shops, in cars, in factories, on the field, in cottages, and in apartment complexes, institute stations of love and guides to love.

God, mold a new, different race kneaded with love.

Transform, Lord, our world into a world of love. Amen.

55

Prayer for the artists

Lord, I meditate on Your transcendent beauty, and I am flooded with a sacred jubilation. I think of You not only as the God of holiness, truth, and love, but also as the God of beauty.

What is our world, God, but a poor reflection, a very small mirage of Your inconceivable and indescribable beauty.

God, we feel that You have greatly honored us by your enabling even us to become creators of beauty. Your heart did not set us up as simple spectators of beauty.

You gave us the sublime joy of creating various forms of beauty.

You gave to certain brothers of ours the special talent to compose music, to paint, to write, to raise up cathedrals. To serve the value of beauty that finds its absolute fulfillment in You.

O You who are without beginning, Eternal Artist, You know how delicate and difficult is the work of the human artist. Therefore I beseech You never to leave them all alone.

Stay always by the side of those brothers and sisters of ours on whom You bestowed the talent of art.

May You be their inspiration. If You leave their side, surely Satan, the king of ugliness, will resume inspiring them. There is no other option.

Help them, You who are *comely in beauty*[51] in the conception of their themes.

Keep far away from their imagination themes that are unproductive, themes that diffuse the odor of despair or corruption. Endow them with a strong sense not only of beauty, but also of holiness and purity. Don't let them disjoin the beautiful from the holy, art from ethics, humanism and truth.

O more than beautiful Creator, make their artwork a performance that will aid life to be enhanced. A window from which a wind of beauty will come, as well as justice and truth.

Please let the artwork be contributive to the wholeness of human beings, let it embellish their souls making them better and happier.

O my God, hold the artist's hand with Your holy hand. Guide it when he writes, sculpts, draws, or composes. Amen.

56

Prayer for our farmers

God, at this very hour as it rains, I lift my spirit to You to thank You. Your rain is so good for us! Our bread depends on it. The livelihood of our farmers depends on it.

Lord, the farmers urgently need Your tender affection. From You, Heavenly Farmer, they wait for suitable weather that will make their work prosperous.

For You are *the one who gives us rain and fruit-bearing seasons from heaven to fill up our hearts with nourishment and cheerfulness.*[52]

You will regulate the coming of the wind and its intensity.

You will bring the seed buried in the earth to life.

You will ripen the fruits, make produce to be abundant, and make the fields sprout.

Lord, give our farmers strength in their toilsome labor.

Lighten their hard labor.
Strengthen their hopes.

Don't bereave them of the joy of seeing their care and worry be rewarded.

Help, O Planter of good things, our farm production be driven forward.

Free the villagers from the interference of wicked people who suck up without any hassle all the sweat and fruits of the labor of those who honorably work off the land.

Lord, don't let a spirit of indignation be harbored in the breasts of outdoorsmen on account of the injustices that befell them.

May it not happen that those who secure our bread go hungry.

Lord, Lord, bless our soil, bless our farmers.

57

Deliver the people from the temptation of suicide

My God, even tonight people will stay awake in the chilly grip of despair. And tonight many souls completely ripped to pieces, lonely in the clutches of the claws of desperation, will wail, groan mournfully, or - alas! - will curse their own lives.

Jesus, I shiver when I reflect on how tonight, maybe even at this moment, hopelessness and dejection will push people towards death. The idea of suicide will besiege many of Your living creatures at different points of the earth.

Giver of Life, don't let this evil come to be.

You came into our world to give eternity's measurements to our lives, the dimensions of eternity.

How does Your heart tolerate the grief of meeting Your little brothers who commit suicide and take violently their lives?

Lord, cancel the designs of the prince of darkness and death.

Free people from the temptation of suicide.

Dissolve the fog of hopelessness.

If You wanted, Lord, You can flood their fatigued souls with the song of life, thus covering over death's requiem.

Let the song of the nightingale resonate in the places where the screech-owl is heard.

Fill, O Lord, their hearts and minds with the desire of life, with the ability and resolution to live, which helps them overcome the wish to die. Show my brethren how suicide is the worst kind of madness, the huge uncorrectable mistake.

Whisper into their hearts words of consolation that never, for any reason, is it too late. That no pain is stronger than our power to endure.

That there is no wound that can't be healed by Your merciful hand.

God, sow hope and faith in You.

Open the roads to life and close forever the paths of death.

58

Prayer for those who are alone and lonely

Lord, You know that many people live in our world all alone. They have no one of their own. They are far from relatives and friends. Or even if they are near relatives, they consider them strangers. They have no one to love them. They are absolutely alone.

They are being wasted away, they are slowly expiring, Jesus, in their isolation. Every day and every night they are shut up too much in their frigid, cruel solitude.

And this could happen, God, at the moment when in our roads, walk or run millions of people! When over six billion people dwell on our planet, there can be so much loneliness!

O All Good, whatever is bad is still worse for these isolated fellow human beings of ours when they experience also Your absence. Alas! There are many people who do not possess enough faith to feel You near them as a Brother and Father.

They live without other people and without God.

And when they happen to get sick or weak, when they are advanced in age, tragedy then takes frightening dimensions for them.

O Incomparable Companion of our lives, Brother and Father, Friend and Maker, resolve this problem and the drama of loneliness that strikes countless numbers of souls.

Introduce brothers and true friends to be with all those who feel or live alone.

Shelter under Your wings, the orphans, the widows, the abandoned people, and the crowd of those whom we fellow human beings have forgotten.

You promised, our Savior, that You will be with us forever, a Living God, *yesterday and today and unto the ages of ages*.[53] We pray particularly that You please visit the lonesome hearts.

May You demolish the walls of solitude made of ice and be a Companion and Loved One to those who being all alone feel faint-hearted.

Heat their existence with Your heart's divine contact.

Lord, become the "You" that millions of people require with an inextinguishable thirst in their lives, the only "You" who can solve the problem and tragedy of loneliness and abandonment.

59

Liberate us from our confusion

Have mercy on us, God, in our confusion. A confusion that embraces everyone and causes everything to become more complicated and scary. Ideas, mentalities, thoughts, feelings, tendencies, and values all are found, Lord, jumbled up and are twisted up in a crazy demon-dance in our own heads. They bring a sort of confusion, an unimaginable impasse.

My God, even the simple people of my neighborhood seem to be lost, they think that the world is close to turning upside-down.

Lord, You see it, our confusion is simply terrible. My God, whatever is bad constantly goes to worse.

The television, the radio, the cinema, the newspaper, the theatre, magazines, books, tourism, all of these things inject us with ideas and ways of behavior.

They connect fragments of the truth with strings of lies, they present diametrically opposed ideologies. They arouse the passions,

Lord, and incite the instincts. They rouse storms in the heart, they cause gaps in our convictions, and they overturn our scale of values.

They distort our "I believe," our Creed.

God, let this Tower of Babel come to its end. Let this condition from now on clear up.

May our convictions become healthy. May Your simple and clear Truth become our faith. May Your Law, All Wise Love, become the fully pure, unshaken start of our lives.

Make Christianity our ideology. Make it a way of thinking for all who today are plagued by the epidemic of confusion.

God, Absolute Simplicity, Perfect Wisdom, remove the impasse of confusion from us.

Give us resilience amidst the ideological influences that cause confusion.

Make us simple and sincere believers, and consistent followers of Your everlasting Truth.

60

A petition for the genius people

Lord, until today I haven't prayed for a specific category of people: for the geniuses.

But now I feel the need to do it. To speak to You, to ask Your favor for these excellent creatures of Yours, whom You endowed with the gift of great intellect.

You gave them the ability, God, to act upon the life and history of our planet. You furnished them with complex, penetrative minds.

Thus they can see and run ahead of their time.

Lord, You wanted the genius to be something distinguished. Therefore, they need special help and preservation on Your part.

Lord, keep the geniuses and exceptionally gifted people under Your direction.

Lead them into a good and profitable use of Your gift. If You leave them, they would perhaps cause harm. Their gift, without the constant intervention of Your wise love, would probably result in a destructive weapon that would exceed every usual boundary.

Have we not seen something like that happening in the past and the present?

God, I beg You, accompany genius with magnanimity, with a deep, great, holy heart.

Keep the geniuses narrowly tied to You, humble, and honest servants of Yours, believers in You.

Use them like chosen instruments that will always intone Your presence.

Like very powerful floodlights, that will illuminate Your road as with a burst of light.

Like resounding trumpets, that will announce Your love and providence.

Lord, make those gifted people pioneers of progress, producers of prosperity for Your world. Establish them as sources of good. Transmitting units of good toward all directions.

61

Protect the young generation

My God, I can't stand it. It provokes distressing feelings in me to see the breaking, the fall of my littlest brothers. God, what an unbearable sensation!

Why do You allow the tender trees to break under the wind's force? Why do buds wither at the hour that they bloom? Why may children lose their innocence succumbing to sin, and may be bound to conditions that cause shame?

O my Maker, until what time will the corruption and trickery of our community break the purity of the youthful generation?

Until when will the children's entrance into adolescence be paid by this inhuman and unethical tax?

Save, All Good Lord, the young blossoms. Defend their priceless purity.

Make the older, riper people not to consider the new generation's compromise with sin and corruption as natural and inevitable.

Save, Almighty God, the children, the adolescents, and the youth from traps. Keep the eyes of their souls always open and watchful.

Protect them from destructive friendships and from bad friends.

Put a trench around their purity and innocence.

Guard the children from ugly, miserable examples of grown-ups. Let the scandals finally stop. Let the agents of the degradation of the youth be neutralized.

And wherever some crack has occurred, wherever someone has fallen, implant wings once again on the youthful soul, so that it will become free by Your grace and lift itself up.

God, I beseech You not only to keep watch over the purity and integrity of them at their tender age, but also to make them strong and radiant.

On the sick and declining world of grown-ups, may the light and good health of youthful purity act benevolently.

Lord, may the lightning bolts of the pure and uncorrupt juvenile spirit cut through the dark chaos of our society.

May suns full of light that shine brilliantly in the children's completely pure eyes illuminate the chaos.

62

Give us good shepherds

Lord, Your people and Your Church implore You: Give us good priests.

Our need for holy shepherds doesn't permit delay.

We need them to teach us Your supernatural truth by example and by their words.

To remind us that there is a heaven above us.

That You exist, the King of another world, where blessedness and harmony walk hand in hand with righteousness and love.

Our souls need the power of enhancing ahead. We long to see the figures of holiness incarnate, men who tamed material nature and the flesh by their strong spirits.

Oh! Let Your priests be people like this!

Let them be *flames of fire*[54] who produce holiness, and convey holiness, and are coaches for virtue.

Don't permit under any circumstance that the ministers of Your Altar become scandals. Don't let them forget their mission.

Make them reflect the heavens, distill serenity and goodness.

Aid them, Lord, help them to solve the problems related to their own lives, so that they aren't harassed or ruined by them. But let them perform their other-worldly work free and undistracted.

Make them Your priests, God, kind, true fathers of our troubled people.

Give them a holy kind of austerity or strictness that is not rough, but friendly and for the good of the people.

Dress them with a kind of tender leniency that doesn't cause slackness or looseness, but strengthens and comforts.

Jesus, let our shepherds be Your copies. Let them live with You and for You, so that they can remind our dull, tired consciences and our sleepy souls of You.

Hear, Eternal Archpriest, our prayer for the priests: Your people and Your Church implore You.

63

Save us from the routine and the boredom

Lord, come to the souls that routine and boredom poison. Save us from these two monsters, which give shape to the face of the days we live in.

You have lived near us, Jesus.

You walked our dust covered roads.

You accompanied us as a man.

You saw with Your human eyes our weaknesses, our wishes, and our outbursts.

You observed whether we could hold up under boredom; if Your creation, while fallen and sinful, could compromise with routine.

Oh! We can't, my Jesus.

Don't You see that many souls choose death, sin, or insanity to save themselves from the nothingness of routine?

How might we endure boredom, Lord? How might fragile human nature not bend under the leaden weight of boredom?

Why don't You intervene? Become for yet another time our Liberator.

Enter our factories and offices.

Visit the cosmopolitan centers, our largest cities, that are lorded over by routine and tediousness.

Stay, Jesus, beside my brothers and sisters who wither away and expire in performing the same mechanical movements hour upon hour.

Show Your bright face to those who all day have to do things with dead, lifeless papers, shut up for years in the same depressing office.

Grant a freedom from routine. Transform work. Give the people new eyes and new hearts.

Jesus, You were tired in the three years of Your liberating work. You deprived Yourself from food and sleep many times so that You could do more good in due time.

Aren't You perturbed, then, at seeing today those people for whom You were crucified get tired from inactivity and tedium?

Come, Lord.

Transform the dead and barren hours of ours into hours of care for our brothers. Give the souls that slowly perish within sloth and tedium the reverberation of Your love.

Push, God, move their hearts.

Stir up the stagnant waters.

Change them into rivers of life.

64

Prayer for my friends

Open Your hands, Lord, and spread out blessings. Take my friends in Your arms, roll them up in light. Warm them with love, furnish them with wisdom.

Make their lives great, peaceful, and worthwhile.

Keep them, God, to be believers in You, just as they have been up to now. And let them stay always fearless as heroes and simple as children. Polite and decisive. Bold and pure.

Lord, let Your gladness dwell in their hearts.

Give them strength of endurance, withstanding pain, and magnanimity in victory.

A calmness in their joy, balanced in successes. Serenity and persistence in misfortunes.

God, I pray for my friends. And at the exact same time I give You my thanks.

Thank You because my friends are one of Your most precious presents to me in my life.

May heaven's blessings and earth's goods shelter, God, my friends.

65

For those about to die

My God, today the bell will toll for many. The cycle of life on earth will come to a close and the cycle of eternity will open.

The last day, Lord, the last hours for thousands of people all over the six inhabited continents.

God, the great unrepeatable moments of their lives are the moments when the echo of death's footsteps are heard on the stairs.

Lord, I pray to You for all those who today give up their spirits. Appear to them clement and merciful.

Let them not go through a rough death.

Let them not expire beaten by the aches of painful diseases.

Nor should their end be sudden and come upon them unprepared.

Lord, please make their hearts ready for the great voyage. Before they close their eyes forever, let them look for You with the everlasting assistance by Confession and Holy Communion. Let them softly whisper a "Lord, have mercy."

Let them say, even though it might be for the first time in their lives, the *"Remember me, Lord, in Your Kingdom."*[55]

My Deliverer, comfort them who today will see one of their dear ones "falling asleep." Let the mystery of death speak to their souls, opening new horizons to life and immortality.

Strengthen the truth that so often gets forgotten: that You are *the Resurrection and the Life.*[56]

Fill the grieving with the happiness to hear Your living words: *Who believes in Me, even if he dies, will live, and everyone who lives and believes in Me will not die again in the age to come.*[57]

Lord, receive in peace and repentance the spirits of our brothers and sisters that today, leaving their corruptible body on earth, will start a new life close to You.

Give them repose in Your blessed arms, O God.

66

Sow freedom on Earth

For me, Omnipotent Lord, the biggest display of Your divinity is Your respect for our freedom.

Before this inconceivable mystery I kneel in adoration, to confess my faith: "I believe in one God, who respects the freedom of His useless servants."

So that You would not break our freedom, You came on earth as a man and were humbled in a way that cannot be understood by our limited mind.

In order to restore our freedom, You were crucified and rose.

And now see. Bend down to our planet, God. See so terrible an amount of servitude!

Look at the millions of slaves.

Barbaric hands of tyrants have strangled and still strangle Your singular divine gift.

Lord, we bury our faces in our hands out of embarrassment whenever we think that our earth contains concentration camps.

We tremble with indignation when we face the hands where the blood still hasn't dried and that constrain human beings by tying them in chains, but which frenziedly crush the freedom of the hearts and murder the independence of the mind.

In the meantime, Lord, You remain silent.

Your silence terrifies us.

Is it possible that out of respect for our freedom You would let tyrants destroy it?

God, grant us immense joy and the unbearable happiness to see servitude demolished in our age.

May no man be subjugated to any other man on the earth.

May there not be lords and slaves.

May no one, absolutely no one, be able to administer or to destroy the freedom of even one man, even though he might be the least of men.

Lord, may our time be a time of the liberation of the slaves.

Fifth Cycle

The Lord said,
"Repent and believe in the Gospel."

Mark 1:15

67

Repent and believe in the Gospel

Lord, You told us, *Repent and believe in the Gospel.*[58]

This is the first, the main condition of a true relationship with You.

We must confess to You that our faith in the Gospel is not very great. So many things of everyday life have beaten and still beat on it. It often seems excessive and unsuitable to us. Often we consider the Gospel very demanding. And then there are hours when it seems to us that the Gospel is a challenge to our logic and intelligence.

Lord, we have difficulty to believe, completely, and without reservations in the Gospel.

But perhaps the reason is found elsewhere. You told us: *Repent and believe in the Gospel.* A great secret is hidden here. The faith in and acceptance of the Gospel presupposes a radical change in thought, in the mentality. A change in the way of facing things, persons, and values. You ask us to repent in order to believe. This is exactly the point of difficulty.

The new, strong wine of Your Gospel demands analogous containers: *Neither do they put new wine into old skins; ...but new wine they put into skins that are new.*[59] Did You not speak thus?

We have to change. We feel that we have to refuse our sinful mentality, our poor rationalism, our narrow minded consideration of things. We have to repent. If You only have given us the power and the decision for such a change!

If You have gifted us with the gift of taking Your words to heart, Lord! If You have placed in our heart and on our lips a "Yes" as the response to Your saying, *"Repent and believe in the Gospel"* ...![60]

68

Become as children

Lord, You told us, *If you do not turn around and become as children, You will never enter into the Kingdom of Heaven.*[61]

You said it so clearly, that You have left us no doubt. So we don't doubt it, but we are scared. And You know why. Forgive us for telling You that this demand of Yours is almost a provocation. If there was a period in history that does everything in order not to allow people to become children, surely it is the time period we live in.

Don't You see, Lord, how hasty is our era in order to make even the children stop being children? Don't You see how quickly it forces children to become grown-ups? So many children's faces have ceased to laugh, long ago. The knowledge of wickedness and the experience gained from the taste of evil wander in the eyes of so many children. When children can't be children, how can youth who are already at a riper age achieve being like children?

But You told us that we must be like children, and Your word does not allow many interpretations, does not allow shortcuts. We have to accept it in its integrity, if we want to be honest Christians. Nothing else remains for us except that we ask simply and sincerely for Your help. Your help, Jesus, so that we may turn around and become *as children*.[62]

This means that You help us feel in all of its importance and correctly this saying of Yours. To desire change wholeheartedly, the turning around that it speaks about.

This means that You help us be brave and bold. In a world that weaves life together with deceit, craftiness, hypocrisy, and disbelief we need daring and bravery for anyone at all to become a child.

And moreover this means that You enlighten us, that we achieve the conjoining of this saying of Yours with the other You said to us: *Become cunning as snakes and honest as doves*.[63] To help us feel that the words "as children" do not mean stupidity and the refusal of using our brains.

We ask these things of You because we want to be consistent with what You ask of us.

69

Prayer for our enemies

Lord, You told us: *Love your enemies*.[64] And You gave us the understanding that this is not a form of exaggeration. It is something that has to be done. This isn't something superfluous. Nor a supplementary addition to Your will, which if we want to we can accept it or reject it.

But, God, here we meet a difficulty. You ask us to love our enemies. But we - and let's be honest at least in front of You - don't really love even our friends very well!

We often deal with these friends as bitter rivals, Lord. They study the same sciences and thus they are our professional rivals. They get high grades while we fail. They accomplish with ease in their studies, while to us everything comes with difficulties. Therefore we are jealous of them; we envy them so easily.

These friends, Lord, also share with us other people's love. And it often seems to us that they get the bigger share. You know how much things like this bother us.

Next, so often our friends irritate us with their words, motions, or a character deficiency that they have.

So often at a time when we are being true and honest with ourselves we feel the need to confess that we don't substantially love our friends, either. If we don't love them, then how may we love our enemies?

Why then do You ask us such things? Why do You ask us to become like athletes in a marathon, when we can't even move our feet?

You surely have Your plan, Omnipotent Lord. By asking us to love our enemies, You help us decide that we should at least love our friends. In the end, You are giving us the chance to love our enemies through our own friends, since our friends are also more or less our rivals.

We feel then that Your saying, *Love your enemies*,[65] must begin with a purification of our love toward our friends. And to move ahead. To go ahead without conditions or limits.

70

Your complaint

Lord, You told us: *You do not want to come to me so that you might have life.*[66] How deeply and painfully Your complaint rings. And with what surprising clarity and accuracy it expresses one of our most tormenting contradictions!

If we thirst for life, You know it a thousand times better than us. The hunger and thirst for life torments us unbearably so often.

We want to live, God.

And while we believe in You - weakly and feebly maybe, but at any rate we do believe in You - we don't come near You. You told us that You are the Life. You are the Life that conquered death. But we don't run near You when we have that spiritual thirst. We look for other fountains to quench our thirst for life. When we come anywhere near You, We know that we will find tranquility and comfort. We don't at all doubt it. But life? Here something makes us stop.

An inconceivable fear takes control of us that the flame of life will be extinguished when we are near You. So finally while we believe, we don't approach You seeking life. And Your complaint remains, *You do not want to come to me so that you might have life.*⁶⁷

We recognize our contradiction. And we ask with all our power for our release from it. Let us enter into the kingdom of Your life.

Give us life, the same life that is lit by Your Resurrection. The same life that moves within the atmosphere of Your immeasurable and limitless love.

Give us life that the Sun of Your joy covers, that the wind of Your freedom refreshingly cools, and that the rivers of Your justice water.

Lord, with outstretched arms we pray: Fill these arms with the treasures of Your life.

71

Seek first the Kingdom of God

Lord, You told us: *Seek first the Kingdom of God.*[68] "Seek first the Kingdom of God."

We feel that in this saying of Yours, You are revealing our guilt. You uncover our heart's wounds. Because - woe to us! - each of us asks in the first place for whatsoever he or she wants, everything except Your Kingdom.

We seek first the material power. The power of money, of position, and of mind.

We seek first for pleasure and comfort, the easy life, and the easy progress. We seek for the least possible amount of toil.

We seek first whatever serves our direct or indirect personal advantage.

We seek first whatever we like, whatever costs us less.

We seek first whatever is connected with ourselves, sadly ready to make pacts even with the Enemy, too, Satan himself.

We seek first...Oh! We feel Your fiery glance scorch us, Lord, to interrupt us: Enough! Surely there won't be an end to this list of things that you seek first. This limitless catalogue, that grows day by day and that forms the reasons for your unhappiness and the rejection of your worth, I contradict with my singular eternal saying: *Seek first the Kingdom of God and His justice and all these things will be given to you.*[69]

How simple and how pure Your truth is, Lord. But how can we get it?

How might we teach our hearts to seek first Your Kingdom and Your justice? How can we get past all these other "firsts", God? No other way than praying to You humbly, simply and with an upright spirit. Lord, we ask first that You teach us, help us, persuade our hearts, wills, and thoughts, to seek first Your Kingdom and Your justice. Amen.

Notes For Scriptural References

1. Luke 11:1
2. Psalms 30:17
3. Ephesians 2:12
4. Psalms 12:4
5. Psalms 88:16
6. Psalms 4:7
7. Luke 17:5
8. Mark 9:24
9. Psalms 129:2
10. Psalms 101:2
11. Psalms 50:1
12 Psalms 129:1
13. Luke 5:20
14. John 5:14
15. James 3:13
16. II Corinthians 1:3
17. Acts 10:38
18. Psalms 7:10
19. Matthew 11:28
20. Matthew 6:9-10
21. Matthew 6:10
22. Matthew 6:13
23. Philippians 4:8
24. Psalms 41:3
25. Matthew 5:8
26. II Timothy 4:5
27. I Timothy 6:12
28. Psalms 69:2
29. John 17:13
30. Romans 1:20
31. Genesis 18:27
32. Psalms 44:3
33. Acts 17:25
34. Psalms 35:10
35. John 8:36
36. Psalms 13:3
37. Matthew 18:3
38. Matthew 6:26
39. Psalms 8:6
40. Psalms 40:4
41. Acts 17:16
42. I John 5:21
43. John 14:6
44. John 14:6
45. John 8:12
46. Matthew 14:17
47. Psalms 30:17
48. Revelation 4:8
49. James 3:17
50. Colossians 2:3

51. Psalms 44:3
52. Acts 14:17
53. Hebrews 13:8
54. Psalms 103:4
55. Luke 23:42
56. John 11:25
57. John 11:26
58. Mark 1:15
59. Matthew 9:17
60. Mark 1:15
61 Matthew 18:3
62. Matthew 18:3
63. Matthew 10:16
64. Matthew 5:44
65. Matthew 5:44
66. John 5:40
67. John 5:40
68. Matthew 6:33
69. Matthew 6:33

Table of Contents

A prologue to the English language Edition

Introduction

First Cycle
1. I don't know how to pray
2. Be the conversant I am looking for
3. Make me feel Your presence
4. Years without prayer

Second Cycle
5. I am thirsty for light
6. Hold my faith upright
7. Forgive me
8. More virtue, more kindness today
9. My behavior tortures me
10. I want so much, I want everything
11. Heal me, please
12. What shall I do about my finances
13. Reveal my real self to me
14. Let me be a warrior for good
15. I want to discuss with You my plans
16. I have been hit by failure
17. I am upset, my God
18. Release me from weariness
19. Everyone is waiting for You
20. The happiness of being able to speak
21. I live among human beings

22. My soul thirsts for the living God
23. Save me from laziness
24. The three agents
25. Save me from the temptations
26. The hunger for happiness tortures me
27. Deliver me from selfishness
28. Stay with me

Third Cycle
29. I give glory to You
30. I praise You for the light
31. You were crucified for me
32. Prayer for the beginning of a new day
33. We bless You because we can think
34. I thank You because I am alive
35. The Hosanna of my freedom
36. I see You in the midst of the storm
37. I thank You for the silence
38. You have shown me a true human being
39. You filled our neighborhoods with children

Fourth Cycle
40. I pray to You on behalf of our world
41. Make our work pleasant
42. Prayer for the families of our neighborhoods
43. Prayer for my parents
44. Prayer for my teachers
45. Forgive those who hurt me
46. Prayer for the sick
47. Prayer for my fellow students
48. Protect us from the idols
49. Reveal Your truth

50. Let hunger be decreased on Earth
51. Prayer for those who work under harsh conditions
52. Prayer for those who deny You
53. Prayer for our scientific workplaces and laboratories
54. Let Your love's rain come
55. Prayer for the artists
56. Prayer for our farmers
57. Deliver the people from the temptation of suicide
58. Prayer for those who are alone and lonely
59. Liberate us from our confusion
60. A petition for the genius people
61. Protect the young generation
62. Give us good shepherds
63. Save us from the routine and the boredom
64. Prayer for my friends
65. For those about to die
66. Sow freedom on Earth

Fifth Cycle
67. Repent and believe in the Gospel
68. Become as children
69. Prayer for our enemies
70. Your complaint
71. Seek first the Kingdom of God

Notes for Scriptural References

His Eminence
Archbishop Demetrios of America

Archbishop Demetrios (Trakatellis) of America was born in Thessaloniki, Greece. In 1950 he graduated with distinction from the University of Athens School of Theology. He was ordained a deacon in 1960, and a priest in 1964.

He was elected Bishop of Vresthena in 1967, auxiliary to the Archbishop of Athens, responsible for the theological education of the clergy. From 1965 to 1971, he studied New Testament and Christian Origins at Harvard University, and was awarded a Ph.D. "with distinction" in 1972. He earned a second doctorate in Theology from the University of Athens "with distinction" in 1977. From 1983 to 1993, he was the Distinguished Professor of Biblical Studies and Christian Origins at Holy Cross Greek Orthodox School of Theology in Brookline, Massachusetts. He also taught at Harvard Divinity School as Visiting Professor of New Testament during the academic years 1984 to 1985 and from 1988 to 1989. In August 1991 he was elevated to be the

Titular Metropolitan of Vresthena. In 2003 he was inducted into the Academy of Athens as a member who resides abroad.

On August 19, 1999, he was elected Archbishop of America by the Holy and Sacred Synod of the Ecumenical Patriarchate. He was enthroned on September 18, 1999 in New York City. In over a decade of leading the Greek Orthodox Archdiocese of America, with more than one and a half million members in the United States, he has touched and inspired the lives of thousands of people with his incessant, methodical and loving archpastoral ministry.

As Exarch of the Ecumenical Patriarchate, he is the Chairman of the Assembly of Canonical Orthodox Bishops of North and Central America. He has been the recipient of many governmental, ecclesiastical, interfaith, and academic honors, both in the USA, Greece and Europe.

Selected Publications of Archbishop Demetrios of America

A Call to Faith: Addresses and Lectures 1999-2003. New York: The Greek Orthodox Archdiocese of America, 2004.

ΑΙΩΝΙΕΣ ΠΑΡΑΔΟΣΕΙΣ (Eternal Traditions). Published in Greek by the Center for Studies of the Holy Monastery of Kykkou, Cyprus, 2010.

Ways of the Lord: Perspectives on Sharing the Gospel of Christ. New York: The Greek Orthodox Archdiocese of America, 2010.

Authority and Passion: Christological Aspects of the Gospel According to Mark. Translated from the Greek by G. Duvall and H. Vulopas. Brookline: Holy Cross Press, 1987.

The Transcendent God of Eugnostos: An Exegetical Contribution to the Study of Gnostic Texts of Nag Hammadi with a Retroversion of the Lost Original Greek Text of Eugnostos the Blessed. Translation of the Doctoral Dissertation at the Theological School of the University of Athens. Translated from the Greek by C. Sarelis. Brookline: Holy Cross Press, 1991.

Being Transformed: Chrysostom's Exegesis of the Epistle to the Romans - A Study. Brookline: Holy Cross Press, 1992.